EMERGENCY!

Emergency!
État d'urgence
Mohamed Hmoudane
Translated by Peter Thompson
Cover and interior art (gravures) by Bouchaïb Maoual
Copyright © 2020 by Peter Thompson and Diálogos Books
Original Copyright © Mohamed Hmoudane
Gravures Copyright © Bouchaïb Maoual
Original publication by Virgule Editions (Tanger), 2016.

Printed in the U.S.A.
First Printing
10 9 8 7 6 5 4 3 2 1   20 21 22 23 24 25

Library of Congress Control Number: 2020936313
Hmoudane, Mohamed
Emergency! / Mohamed Hmoudane;
with Peter Thompson (translator)
and Bouchaïb Maoual (gravures)
p. cm.
ISBN: 978-1-944884-78-9

DIÁLOGOS
dialogosbooks.com

Acknowledgements

Mohamed Hmoudane, Bouchaïb Maoual, Rachid Khaless
and Bill Lavender have worked together to make this
a beautiful book. I'm indebted to the first three for
permission, and to the last for elements of design—both
for the present publication and for the future of American
publishing. A sabbatical leave from Roger Williams
University was also instrumental.

Preface

Mohamed Hmoudane is a prominent Moroccan poet (principally), novelist and translator, and is among those—like the widely-known Abdellatif Laâbi—who live in France. With this book, there is some question of Hmoudane's precarious "destiny," as one of his characters calls it in *French Dream*—that is, if he still lived in Morocco. If that is overstating the "emergency" (after all, the book was published without incident in Morocco), still we must recognize its assault not only on violent and purblind religious fundamentalism but also on the state (the French title of this book translates as *State* of Emergency) of Moroccan civil society: suspenseful, polemically charged, tilting between expressive and repressive.

So much in Morocco is starkly binary: Muslim and Christian, urban and *montagnard,* revolutionary (from the 1956 push for independence and the Istiqlal party) and ultra-traditional, Berber and Arab, arabophone and francophone, the reading populace and the 47% illiterate, men's roles and the position of women. The contemporary Mohamed Loakira, a bit older than Hmoudane, has sharpened this dualism in looking at Arab Spring (*et se voile le printemps…*; English title *and the spring is veiled over…*, Diálogos, 2017). Drawing on folklore, Islamic legend and history, much as Hmoudane does, he looks at spring, 2011 as a two-faced God, one of both hope and eventual betrayal. Another rich contrast: Loakira's texts often reveal him to be a devout Muslim, while *Emergency!* (whatever Hmoudane's personal spiritualism) is a frontal attack on Islamic sectarianism and fanaticism.

Even under a monarchy—one that has recently grown somewhat less tolerant—and amid police surveillance and sometimes harsh repression, there are pockets of strength in the Moroccan publishing scene. Newspapers debate issues openly and sometimes criticize the government (not the same thing as criticizing the royals). Exposés of the previous king's regime pile up in bookstores. And, while Hmoudane could have published this book in France (he publishes with Seuil, L'Harmattan and the recently folded but important La Différence), he published it in Morocco with a bold upstart editor. This house, Virgule Editions, bears watching. Along with Loakira's work, and major writers such as Abdelaziz Mansouri, it has brought out provocative story collections such as Essam-Eddine Tbeur's *Rires et insignifiance* à *Casablanca* and (founding editor of Virgule) Rachid Khaless's *Absolut hob*. Loakira's *La Nuit des disgraciés* also shines a harsh light on religious fanaticism, and was published in Morocco (by Marsam).

Another positive sidelight is that English-language publishers are finally open to working with translations beyond those of the best-selling novelist Tahar ben Jelloun. Several of Laâbi's works are available in English, Ghita El Khayat is in five languages, and the dazzling novelists Ahmed Buonani and Mohammed Khaïr-Eddine (almost completely unknown in the West) are just this year appearing in English.

I do not know. In the end, when I re-read the word destiny that slipped onto the page (above) without my really

thinking the word, if I should melt in tears or laugh out
loud, leaping idiotically and banging my head against
the wall—it would be best to alternate laughter and tears
while wincing—because this word is so associated in my
mind with greatness, glory, immortality. It is inappropriate
to call "destiny" a bitch of a life led unleashed from day
to stumbling day, much of which evaporates in squalid
bars— "rat holes," "delinquent havens," "places of moral
disease"—in shit jobs, when I manage to find one, writhing
in a void, in a void...
(*French Dream*, Editions de La Différence, 2005; my
translation; though the title is English, the book is in
French).

Here Hmoudane's novelistic persona describes his
"destiny" as "a dog's life." And what the poet suggests as
the grand connotation of "destiny" is, for writers of his
generation, the large picture of post-colonial life: sometimes
an exile, sometimes a chosen struggle in France or Spain.
This is also Morocco's destiny, and the present incarnation
of colonialism, that is, the unwholesome miasma of neo-
colonialist connections to France. Hundreds of North African
writers have touched on this subject, with Ben Jelloun
specifically describing the destiny of immigrant workers
in France (*Les Yeux baissés,* Seuil, 1991), and Nabile Farès
evoking (with linked poems) women "boat-people" trying
to reach Europe (*Exile: Women's Turn*, Diálogos, 2017). The
following is addressed to both France and to the king of
"the Years of Lead," Hassan II: "Alas, a thousand times alas,
I'm weak, fallible, and above all very little inclined to be
thankful—as I ought—to my benefactors" (*Le Ciel, Hassan
II et Maman France*, Editions de La Différence, 2010).What
we take from this is that Hmoudane is a contemporary who

turns a hard eye on the post-colonial world, and spares none of its deceptions, splits in consciousness, demographic divisions. Not all North African writers choose this focus, nor do the majority simultaneously find their targets in Africa and in the grittiest neighborhoods of Europe.

And then there is this book, *Emergency!*, whose poetry is ethereal, rising above the substantives of squalor while still engaging the touch-stones of polemic:

I see
[...]
Blood neighing and
Stirred by dissonance
And I dance
Wallowing in it
With today's cadavers

The book maintains a tone that is scriptural, prophetic, the tone of a Jeremiad. What Laâbi calls Hmoudane's "strange ceremony of the word." This is not simply the elevated tone of poetry generally, but a voice lifted in censure. And it reminds us that Arabic (though this book was written in French) has several registers, including a tone and syntax in classical Arabic that is appropriate for scripture and myth. And at the same time:

With ink weighed like anchor
Distilled
Drunk to the dregs
You'll see me wander
In impossible cities
You'll see me adrift
On a heaving sea
With dreams aflame

Hmoudane wants to inveigh against religious fanatics in a language that is airy and often abstract, somewhat like the intangible imagery of Ahmed Barakat (a Moroccan, roughly contemporary with Hmoudane but deceased, who wrote in Arabic; cf. *A Body That Must Rest On Air*, Mindmade Books, 2008). It is as if he wants either to sustain himself above the fray, or to elevate himself to a hieratic or prophetic position—a power position that invokes and catalyzes change.

In this way Hmoudane assumes the burden and the debility of all poets: to be in the right, to know Platonic truth, to see further than others do, and yet to do so only with words, with evanescent imagery. And still it is this phanopoeia, these apparitions, that have beguiling and lasting power. They are the poetic art that interests this translator.

Blood, crystal, and cadavers surge among the less concrete dreams, shadows, tribes. Hard symbols dissolve to emblems, themes dissolve to tropes. As with much modern poetry, the abstract does an unresolved dance with the concrete, rather than complementing it in a logical construction. And this is how, with Hmoudane, ancient sectarianism and swordsmanship in the Middle East become transcendent. The poems achieve a suspended time between the past and the Arab world's problematic future. The mix of proper names, invective and polemic (through obvious logical jumps and anachronism) become a message no less assertive than the piety of Bilal or Othman: we are overwhelmed by the fragility and absurdity of history's message, and by the spoof of its overlay on modern society. A good part of poetry's essence—transformational, metaphorical—

is this dissolving of one message into another, one mode of speech into another, one stark noun into another. So that "message"—or hypotactic "meaning"—as a finality crumbles and its parts (here fundamentalist, historical, revolutionary) are liberated and vital.

And a giant share of the pleasure of translating such work is dropping the English nouns into their places—both on the concrete side and on the abstract—and seeing them enlist themselves in this process.

—Peter Thompson

Note: A Glossary of less familiar terms follows the text, pp. 108-9.

Mohamed Hmoudane

EMERGENCY!

État d'urgence

Translated by
Peter Thompson

Gravures by
Bouchaïb Maoual

DIÁLOGOS
BOOKS
New Orleans

No more words. I inter the dead in my belly. Shouts, drum, dance, dance, dance, dance!

Rimbaud

As for the poets, only the wayward follow them. Don't you see them, wandering in the valleys and speaking those things they do not do?

Koran

Ignorance leads to fear, fear leads to hate and hate promotes violence. Such is the equation.

Averroès

When it comes to money, the whole world has the same religion.

Voltaire

À Jihane, Katia et Mehdi

for Jihane, Katia and Mehdi

Je danse bardé de blessures
Avec des cadavres depuis
Ma bouche dégoulinant de sons
Les morts comme les mots
Répandent fumée et cendre
Sur la chaussée tapissée
De douilles et de lambeaux
De chair dépecée ·
Je danse en cognant mes ombres
Contre les vitrines éclaboussées
De gyrophares et de sang
Vibrant à force de sirènes
Je danse comme égorgé à l'assaut
De la nuit j'ameute et enrôle
Les astres

I dance sheathed in wounds
And with corpses and from
My mouth sounds dribbling
The dead are like words
They spread smoke and ash
Over a roadway padded
With bullet shells and shreds
Of severed flesh
I dance bumping my shadows
On windows spattered
By blood and flashing lights
Shivering in the blast of sirens
I dance like a throat-slit leaping
On the night I call forth and enlist
The stars

À l'orée de l'aube
Imminente
Par des marches sculptées
Peu importe dans quelle
Évanescente idée
De granit ou de marbre
Je descends en remontant
Les siècles vers des cités enfouies
Sous un alphabet de sable
Semé par les vents
Soufflant au gré de ma gorge

At the glint of the imminent
Dawn
Over sculpted steps
In no matter what
Evanescent idea
Of granite or of marble
I descend back through
The centuries toward buried cities
Under an alphabet of sand
Sown by the winds
Puffing to my throat's desire

Encre levée
Distillée
Bue à la lie
Vous me verrez errer
Dans d'impossibles villes
Vous me verrez voguer
Sur un océan houleux
De songes enfiévrés
Vous me verrez dire
Ce que je n'aurai jamais fait
Vous me verrez égarer
Davantage les égarés
Qui me suivent partout
De toute éternité

With ink weighed like anchor
Distilled
Drunk to the dregs
You'll see me wander
In impossible cities
You'll see me adrift
On a heaving sea
With dreams aflame
You'll see me speak
Those things I've never really done
You'll see me lead further astray
The wayward
Who follow me everywhere
Through all eternity

Saccagées les stèles
Hiératiques
Anéanties les idoles
Maléfiques
Vaincus usuriers
Et négociants
J'entre à La Mecque
Escorté par l'Archange
À la tête d'une armée
De troubadours
Tambourins à la main
Chanter la paix scellée
Par le Verbe Divin
Le sang des martyrs
Et les compromis

The hieratic stele
Plundered
Malefic idols
Annihilated
The usurers routed
With the merchants
I come unto Mecca
Escorted by the Archangel
At the head of an army
Of troubadours
Long drums under their arms
To sing out the peace sealed
By Divine Word
By the newly pledged
And the blood of the martyrs

Appelle frère Abyssin
Avec ta voix d'ébène
À la nouvelle aube
Montée avec ce cortège
De soleils prompts à éclater
Des abysses de l'humanité
Appelle frère Abyssin
Avec ta voix cristalline
À la nouvelle fraternité
Nous enterrons à jamais
La hache de guerre
Maintenant que Dieu
A accompli ses serments
Psalmodie frère Abyssin
À pleins poumons
Avec ta voix épurée :
Quiconque entrera dans la demeure d'Abu Sofiane
Sera en sécurité
Quiconque fermera sa porte sur lui-même
Sera en sécurité
Quiconque entrera à la mosquée
Sera en sécurité…

Abyssinian brother call out
In your ebony voice
To the new dawn
Climbing
From humanity's abyss
With its cortège of suns ready to burst
Call out Abyssinian brother
In your voice of crystal
To the new brotherhood
Forever
We're burying the hatchet
Now that God has fulfilled his vows
Give forth hymns Abyssinian brother
Full-breathed
In that rarified voice:
Whoever enters the dwelling of Abu Sufyan
Will be safe
Whoever closes the door on himself
Will be safe
Whoever enters the mosque
Will be safe...

Emporté par ton chant
Extatique
Depuis le sommet
De la Kaaba habillée
Dans quelques siècles
D'une kiswa satinée
Entièrement confectionnée
En dollars américains
Entouré de tous les Prophètes
Je laisse en legs aux tribus
La somme de mes songes

Carried aloft by chanting
Ecstatic
From the top
Of the Kaaba in recent centuries
Draped in its satiny *kiswa*
Confected entirely
Of American dollars
And surrounded by all the Prophets
I leave in bequest to the tribes
The sum of all my dreams

Ombre démultipliée
De moi-même
De danses en accidences
J'entre à Médine
Instituer l'Assassinat
Orchestrer le saccage
Le carnage
Le festin de sang
L'orgie de cadavres
L'immense *fitna*

A shadow delegated
From myself
From dance to haphazard
I enter Medina
To set up the Assassination
Orchestrate the plunder
The carnage
The banquet of blood
Cadaver orgy
The immense *fitna*

Que chaque glaive brandi
Se réclamant de mes songes
S'en abreuve jusqu'à l'enivrement
À nourrir le grand embrasement
À fendre le ciel
À pulvériser les astres
En une infinité de métaphores
Tracées sur le sable du désert
En lettres nomades
Serpentant une à une
Dune après dune
Dans le sillage des caravanes
Et des razzias
Du Yémen au Levant
D'Antioche à Chang'an ...

May every sword brandished
And speaking for my dreams
Drink unto drunkenness
To feed the great blaze
Split the sky
Pulverize the stars
In infinite metaphors
Sketched on desert sand
In nomad letters
Snaking one by one
From dune to dune
In the wake of caravans
And slave-raids far
From Yemen to the Levant
Antioch to Chang'an...

Je vois
Survolant le champ de bataille
Avec les essaims d'oiseaux
Crachant les uns après les autres
Des boules de marne pétries
Du feu de la géhenne
À travers la poussière étincelante
La Mère des Croyants
Naguère absoute par la Révélation
Fantomale dans son palanquin
Juché sur un chameau
Exhorter de toute son absence
Un clan de ses enfants
À appliquer la loi tribale du talion
Pour Dieu et son trône ici-bas
Jadis tout en lumière
Souillé à présent de giclures
De cervelles
De sang
D'excréments ...

I see
Winging above the battlefield
With flocks of birds
Spitting one by one
Balls of clay fired
In the flames of Gehenna
Through the glinting dust
I see the Mother of All Believers
Lately absolved by the Revelation
Spectral in her palanquin
Perched on a camel
And exhorting with her full absence
A clan of her children
To apply the tribal law of retaliation
For God and his throne here below
Aglow in days of yore
Now spattered with gouts
Of brain
Of blood
Of excrement...

Je vois
Dans le déferlement
Tumultueux des cavaliers
Et des cadavres dardés
Rouler les têtes tranchées
Sous les sabots des juments
Enflammées
La cavalcade de feu
Rompre le pacte clanique
Et emporter dans un gigantesque
Tourbillon de flammes
Les parchemins coraniques
D'Uthman
À chaque battement
De paupières
Mes yeux à force de voir
Éjaculent
En même temps que Dieu
L'encre chaotique de la Création
Des vermines noires
Giclant comme du sang
Sur la page

I see
In the knights' tumultuous
Unfurling
And the skewered bodies
Severed heads rolling
Beneath the hooves of mares
Aflame
I see the cavalcade of fire
Break the pact of clans
And carry off in a gigantic
Whirlwind of flames
The Koranic parchments
Of Uthman
With each beat
Of my eyelids
My eyes by dint of staring
Ejaculate
Along with God
The chaotic ink of the Creation
Black vermin
Trickling like blood
Over the page

Je vois
Au-delà des confins
De l'empire à bâtir
Et de l'Histoire
Hennir le sang attisé
De la discordance
Et je danse
En y pataugeant
Avec les cadavres d'aujourd'hui
Et ceux à venir

I see
Out beyond the borders
Of the empire to come
Beyond history too I see
Blood neighing and
Stirred by dissonance
And I dance
Wallowing in it
With today's cadavers
And those that lie ahead

Je vois
Jusqu'à la cécité
Et je danse à tâtons
Au roulement assourdissant
Des tambours
Aux cris déchirants
Des morts
Aux mots à jamais
Étouffés

I see
Unto blindness
And dance feeling my way
To the deafening roll
Of drums
The rending cries
Of the dead
And words forever
Stifled

Voici se déverser les versets
Depuis le Coran arboré
Transpercé par les lances
Croisées des frères ennemis
Sur le sol assouvi de cadavres
Enivré de sang
Voici l'Imam observer
Une prière mortuaire
Devant son propre cadavre
Installé sur le trône de l'Éternité
La tête coiffée d'un diadème
Incrusté de soleils noirs
Et de perles ensanglantées
Dans la grande mosquée d'Al Kûfa
À sa droite les fidèles
Drapés dans la nuit
Chantent en pleurs sa geste
Sa céleste gloire
Sa future résurrection
À sa gauche les dissidents
Prêtent allégeance à la mort
À jamais

Now see the stanzas spilling
From the Koran hoisted up
And pierced by the crossed
Lance of brothers become enemies
Pouring over ground sated with corpses
Drunk with blood
Here is the Imam observing
Funerary prayer
Before his own cadaver
Installed on Eternity's throne
The diadem that coifs it
Is encrusted with black suns
And bloody pearls
In the great Al Kufa Mosque
On the body's right the faithful
Cloaked in night
Sing his rite with weeping
His glory in heaven
His future resurrection
On his left the dissidents
Give allegiance to death
Ever after

Les voici tenir conseil
À Ctésiphon
Et le serment de destituer
Du majestueux trône
Le somptueux cadavre
Appelé à la résurrection
D'exterminer jusqu'au dernier
Partout tous les apostats
De couper à la racine
Pour toujours
Le cheveu de Muawiya

Here they are holding council
At Ctesiphon
And vowing to hurl down
From that majestic throne
The sumptuous cadaver
Summoned to the resurrection
To exterminate in every place
Apostates unto the last one
To sever at the root
And forever
Muawiya's strand of hair

Porté par l'écho
Entaché de sang
Chargé de menaces
De fulminations
J'entre à Damas
Pavoisée d'oriflammes
Brodés de peste noire
Assister aux épousailles ·
Célébrées en grande pompe
Entre le printemps
Et la Nuit

Borne by the echo
Smeared with blood
Burdened with threats
And fulminations
I enter a Damascus
All decked with gonfalons
Embellished by buboes
To attend the marriage
Fêted with such pomp
Between spring
And the Night

Voici scintiller
Dans les splendides jardins
De la Ghouta
Les nigelles de sang
Comme les crânes
Au bout des lances
Alignées sur l'esplanade
Tout en carrare
De la grande mosquée

And here glinting
In the splendid gardens
Of La Ghouta
Love-in-a-mist of blood
Like skulls
At the tips of lances
Lined up on the Carrara marble
Of the great mosque's
Esplanade

Sous un ciel crépusculaire
Piqué d'astres apocalyptiques
En déroute
Stellaires des vents
Incendiaires
Balayent le Coran
Brûlent les versets
En dispersent la cendre
Aux quatre points cardinaux
Les anges et les démons sonnent
Par fatwas interposées
La prophétie enfin réalisée
En cette terre bénie du Levant
Tant chérie par l'Élu :
La dissolution des Nations
La Fin des Temps

Under a twilight sky
Pricked by a shambles
Of apocalyptic stars
Winds stellar
And incendiary
Sweep away the Koran
And burn its every strophe
Spreading the ashes
To the four points of the compass
Angels and demons ring out
In overlapping fatwas
The prophecy come to pass
In this blessed stretch of the Levant
So beloved of the Chosen One:
Nations' dissolution
And the End of Time

J'embarque par je ne sais
Quel engrenage syllabique
De mots ciselés comme
Par des lames météoritiques
Transparentes
Avec les Qarmates
Sur un bateau attelé
À Saturne et Jupiter
Conjugués
Le long de l'Euphrate
Crû par les larmes et le sang
Cap sur un immense chant
Funéraire

I embark through a nameless
Syllabic clockwork
Of words chiseled as if
By transparent
Meteorite blades
Along with the Quarmates
On their boat
Towed by Saturn and Jupiter
Who are mated
For the length of the Euphrates
As it swells with tears and blood
The prow set
On the immense chant
Of a funeral

Précédé par un torrent de hennissements
À moins que ce ne soit une averse
De bétyles ou d'obus
J'entre à Alep
Annoncer la bonne nouvelle
De mon propre avènement
Depuis les minarets et les clochers
Et de barricade en tranchée

Preceded by a storm of neighing
Unless it were a shower
Of bombshells and baetyli
I enter Aleppo
To proclaim the good news
Of this my advent
From minaret and bell tower
And every trench and barricade

Je ferme alors comme à Al-Hasa
Toutes les mosquées
Ensevelis à jamais Moïse
Jésus et Mahomet
Restitue aux déshérités
La Pierre Noire et l'or pillé
Ébauche par le feu et le sang
La future alliance
Entre le marteau et la faucille

And so I close down as at Al-Hasa
All the mosques
Bury forever Moses
Jesus and Mohamed
Restore to the disinherited
The Black Stone and the plundered gold
I sketch out in fire and blood
The future alliance
Of hammer and sickle

Par les Tables de Lois effritées
Les Saintes Écritures
Et le Coran effacés
Par l'éternelle vacance du trône
Divin et khalifal
Par ma danse démentielle
Ma danse imamienne
Ma danse cérémonielle
Pour le nouvel Orient
Tant attendu

By the crumbling Tablets of Commandments
The Holy Scriptures
And Koran all erased
By the divine and caliphal
But eternally vacant throne
By my demented dance
My imam's dance
My ceremonial dance
For the long-awaited
New Orient

À Samarra
Du sommet du minaret en spirale
Comme jadis Bilal à la prière
J'appelle les Zanj à l'insoumission
À irriguer avec le sang noir
La terre d'islam
Qu'il y pousse à l'ombre d'Allah
Des vergers d'ambre et de rubis

At Samarra
From high on the spiral minaret
Like Bilal of yore at prayer
I call on the Zanj to rise up
Irrigate with black blood
The land of Islam
That there might grow in Allah's shadow
Orchards of ruby and amber

À Samarra
Du sommet du minaret en spirale
Comme jadis Spartacus à Rome
Les esclaves gladiateurs
J'appelle les Zanj à la révolte
À tracer avec le glaive
Trempé dans le sang noir
Sur le linceul de la foi
Et les planches palimpsestiques de loi
L'alphabet de la délivrance

At Samarra

From the top of the spiral minaret

As did Spartacus back in Rome

To the gladiator slaves

I call forth the Zanj in revolt

To limn with sabers

Soaked in black blood

On the burial shroud of faith

And palimpsest tables of the law

The alphabet of deliverance

Est-ce le bruit de mes chaînes
Ou est-ce le son dissident des crotales
De l'incommensurable deuil
Sont-ce les cris des femmes
Violées
Leurs larmes tombées en cataractes
Ou est-ce le tumulte de l'Euphrate déchaîné
Que j'entends
Marchant les yeux bâillonnés vers l'échafaud
Vers ma décapitation
....
Et le bourreau de psalmodier la sentence :
Je vois des têtes qui ont bourgeonné, mûres à être
cueillies ...
Et cette foule qui sait bien faire foule
Pour peu qu'elle le veuille de brailler :
Allah est grand !
Au diable les hérétiques !
Au diable les mécréants !

Is this the sound of my chains
Or the dissident noise of the rattlesnakes
Of immeasurable mourning
Are these the cries of women
Raped
An the cataracts of their tears
Or is it the roar of the Euphrates unchained
In my ear
As I walk blindfolded to the block
And my decapitation
....
And the executioner chanting my sentence:
I see heads that have sprung up, ripe
for harvesting...
And then this crowd ready to mob up
At any pretext, ready always to bawl:
Allah is great!
To the devil with the heretics!
To the devil with the wrongdoers!

Roulez tambours

Sonnez trompettes

Chantez larmes

La Passion du Petit-fils

Ô Hussein

À Karbala

J'allume le feu

Autour de ton cercueil

Noyé dans le sang

Je bois les flammes

Comme un poison réconfortant

Dans ton crâne

Devenu coupe

Passée de main en main

Par les imams cachés

En secrète procession

Dans la cour omeyyade

De la nuit damascène

Empestant le meurtre

Jusqu'à l'apocalyptique

Apparition

Roll on drums
Trumpets sound
And tears sing out
The Grandson's passion
Oh Hussein
At Karbala
I light the fires
Around your sepulcher
Drowning in blood
I drink flames
Like a soothing poison
From your skull
Become goblet
And passed hand to hand
By imams hidden
In secret procession
Through the Ommayad court
Of a Damascene night
That reeks of murder
All the way to the apocalyptic
Advent

Par la porte du Désastre
Sertie des douze astres
J'entre à Bagdad
Accueilli par une foule en deuil
Pleurant en se flagellant
L'imam et sa descendance
Ô Ali ô Hassan ô Hussein
J'appelle en guise de prière
Du souvenir à une immense danse
Jusqu'à orgasmer à l'unisson
De l'ultime Mahdi et des Hachichines
De guerre intestine
En guerre intestine
De la mer à la mer
Jusqu'aux siècles des siècles

Through the gate of disaster
Studded with a dozen stars
I enter Baghdad
Greeted by a mourning mob
Flagellating and weeping
The Imam and his descendants
Oh Ali Oh Hassan Oh Hussein
I call out as a kind of prayer
From a memory to the vast dance
And collective orgasm
From the last Mahdi and the Hashish Cult
From civil war
To civil war
From sea to sea
Unto centuries and their centuries

Franchi le miroir
Traversées mes ombres
Comme autant de voies
Escarpées
Tracées avec une encre
Translucide au gré de mes pas
J'entre à Cordoue
Architecturée par le Coran
Le miel et le vin coulent à flots
Comme dans les jardins d'Eden
Déjà
Goutte à goutte distillé
De quelque alambic hellénique
Allah en de somptueuses
Noces épouse la Raison
Avant que les Ténèbres
Ne l'épousent

Mirror passed through
My shadows crossed over
Like so many steep
Paths
Traced in translucent ink
At the will of my footsteps
I enter Cordoba
Of Koranic design
Honey and wine flow in wavelets
As in old
Eden
Drop by drop gathered
In some Hellenic still
Allah in sumptuous
Ceremony marries Reason
Before the Darkness
Can take him for spouse

Et soudain j'entends
Martelant les sentences
De son gourou
Croasser d'une voix calomniatrice
Placide
Manichéenne
Le ductile instrument du crime
L'inusable soldat du creative chaos
L 'Ange de l'Apocalypse
Conçu dans les éprouvettes
Des think tanks aseptisés
Béni par les dieux de la Bourse
Et les oligarques
Et les marchands de canons
Et les clones pullulants
D'Ibn Taymiyya
À la botte des émirs de pacotille
Tant il demeure
Dans l'obscur poker
Derrière les lourds rideaux
De fumée
De quelque manière qu'ils battent
Les cartes à tous les coups
Le meilleur joker :

And suddenly I hear
Hammering out the maxims
Of his guru
Cawing in a slanderous voice
A placid
Manichaean voice
The malleable instrument of crime
Indestructible soldier of creative chaos
The Angel of The Apocalypse
Conceived in the test tubes
Of antiseptic think tanks
Blessed by the gods of the Stock Market
And the oligarchs
The cannon mongers
And the swarming clones of
Ibn Taymiyya
Sucking up to third-rate emirs
As he remains
In the shadowy round of poker
Behind heavy curtains
Of smoke
No matter how with every hand
they shuffle the cards
The finest joker:

« Allah est Lumière
Éternelle
Allah est grand
N'en déplaise aux traîtres
Endogamiques
Apostats de ta trempe
Frères siamois
De Satan
Suppôts de Juda
De Rome
Des Croisés
De Sykes-Picot... »

"Allah is Eternal
Light
Allah is great
With all due respect to endogamous
Traitors
Apostates of your caliber
Siamese twins
To Satan
Henchmen of Judah
Of Rome
Of the crusaders
Of Sykes-Picot..."

Et le combattant du nouveau khalifat fantasmé
Lumpen-terroriste biberonné aux jeux vidéo
Abruti béat frais émoulu de quelques caves
D'obédience wahhabite à la périphérie
De l'Histoire et des métropoles
Bardé de rudiments théologiques
Et d'une poignée de mots en arabe
De s'empresser juste avant de semer la mort
De poster son selfie
Kalachnikov en bandoulière
Sur fond de fresque rehaussée
D'un drapeau noir célébrant
« Les valeureux guerriers d'antan
De la glorieuse oumma »
Dans l'idyllique royaume de Zuckerberg
Index levé
En hommage à l'Unique
Large sourire arboré
Clin d'oeil aux houris promises
Bradées à coups de versets
Savamment distillés
Rabâchés à n'en plus finir ...

And the fighter in the new fantasy caliphate
Lumpen-terrorist with video games for a baby bottle
Dazed benighted freshly graduated from a cave somewhere
Wahhabi adherent on the periphery
Of history and the centers of civilization
Armored with theological rudiments
And a handful of Arabic words
So attentive just before sowing death
To post a selfie
Kalashnikov hanging on his chest
On a backdrop of fresco set off
By a black flag celebrating
"The valiant warriors of yore
In the glorious Ummah"
In the idyllic kingdom of Zuckerberg
Index finger raised in homage to Oneness
Sporting a wide smile
With a wink to those promised virgins
Sold off for verses recited
The Koran wisely distilled
And mumbled without end…

Je danse bardé de blessures

Avec des cadavres depuis

Ma bouche dégoulinant de sons

À Lahore   Les morts comme les mots

À Paris   Répandent fumée et cendre

À Istanbul   Sur la chaussée tapissée

À Madrid   De douilles et de lambeaux

À Homs   De chair dépecée

À Mossoul   Je danse en cognant mes ombres

À Djakarta   Contre les vitrines éclaboussées

À Bruxelles   De gyrophares et de sang

À Casablanca Vibrant à force de sirènes

À Kaboul...   Je danse comme égorgé à l'assaut

De la nuit j'ameute et enrôle

Les astres

I dance sheathed in wounds
And with corpses and from
My mouth sounds dribbling
In Lahore   The dead are like words
Paris   They spread smoke and ash
Istanbul   Over a roadway padded
Madrid   With bullet shells and shreds
Homs   Of severed flesh
Mosul   I dance bumping my shadows
Jakarta   On windows spattered
Brussels   With blood and flashing lights
Casablanca   Shivering in the blast of sirens
Kabul   I dance like a throat-slit leaping
On the night I call forth and enlist
The stars

Par l 'imminence de l'aube
Par le soleil en phase
De percer l'épaisse coque
De la nuit
Puisse-t-il en jaillir fulgurant
Et noyer l 'obscurité
Dans sa diluvienne lumière
Partout et nulle part
Je danse bardé de blessures
Avec des cadavres
Sur la macabre symphonie
Des voitures piégées
Accouplée de rafales
De balles tirées
À tout bout de champ
Assortie de cris
Comme autant de refrains
D'un chant tragique
Allant crescendo
Porté au firmament
Par les larmes et le sang
Déchaînés résonnant
Comme un ouragan
De violons

Through dawn's imminence
Through the sun's announcing
And its piercing the thick shell
Of night
May it spring forth blazing
To drown the dark
In torrential light
Everywhere and nowhere
I dance armored with wounds
With cadavers
Above the macabre symphony
Of car bombs
Joined by gales
Of bullets fired
From every direction
Raising cries
Like so many refrains
Of a tragic song
In crescendo
Lifted on high
By tears and blood
Unchained and resonating
Like a hurricane
Of violins

Soudain dans mes bras
Schéhérazade clochardisée
Tout en loques
Pieds nus
Cheveux ébouriffés
Visage défiguré
La chair criblée de vis
D'écrous
De clous
Me somme en agonisant
De rapporter le récit de son errance
De son rapt
De son interminable séquestration
De son viol
De sa folie
De son imminente disparition

Suddenly in my arms
Scheherazade like a bag-lady
All in rags
Barefoot
Hair wild
Disfigured
Her flesh shot through with screws
Bolts
Nails
She summons me as she dies
To bear the tale of her wandering
Her abduction
Endless captivity
Rape
Her madness
And imminent disappearance

Les tapis ne volent plus
Le rêve n'a plus d'ailes
La fantaisie emmurée
La nuit ne donne plus
Naissance au jour
La nuit nichée pour toujours
Dans les coeurs et les esprits

Magic carpets fly no more
Dream no longer has wings
With fantasy walled up
Night no longer gives birth
To the day
Night burrowing forever
In heart and mind

Ferme tes yeux Schéhérazade
Puisses-tu ne pas voir les sordides
Affiches frappées de ton sexe
Et ma tête mis à prix
Placardées sur les murs de ce bazar
Devenu mosquée
Et de cette mosquée devenue bazar
Où l'obscène ignorance
Se déguise en prude piété
Où les marchands et les prédicateurs
Prostituent Dieu et sa parole
Où le paradis se négocie
Comme s'il était un vulgaire tapis
Mais au prix fort du sang

Close your eyes Scheherazade
And be blind to the sordid
Posters of your crotch
And of the price on my head
Plastered on the walls of this bazar
Now a mosque
Or this mosque become bazar
Where obscene ignorance
Is masked as prudish piety
Where merchants and preachers alike
Prostitute God and his word
Where paradise is bargained
Like a cheap rug
But at the high price of blood

Prends pour la route
Schéhérazade
Quelques dernières rasades
D'alcool à brûler
Puissent-elles t'aider à supporter
Ton vagabondage
Dans les sombres sentiers
De la mort

For the road
Scheherazade
Take a few glasses
Of fire water
May they help you bear
The hapless wandering
The shadowy paths
Of death

Meurs en paix maintenant
Schéhérazade
J'oindrai
En guise d'ablution funéraire
Ta dépouille de papier
De ma bave
De mon sang
De mon sperme
De mon encre
Je t'inhumerai dans mon verbe
Puisses-tu continuer à rêver
Comme dans mon sommeil
Pour l'éternité
Plus mille et une nuits

Now die in peace
Scheherazade
I will anoint
As with funeral ablutions
Your paper remains
With my drool
My blood
My sperm
My ink
I will bury you in my words
That you might go on dreaming
As in my own sleep
For eternity
Plus a thousand and one nights

À l'ombre de ton ombre
Sur les ruines des cités
Je danse bardé de blessures
Avec ton cadavre évanescent depuis
Ma bouche dégoulinant de sang
Ma langue tranchée tente
L'indicible tandis que les sirènes
Hurlent de concert l'état d‹urgence
Dans la banlieue aux allures de ghetto
Je me fonds dans la brume
Mouillé par le halo des néons
Sous l'enseigne du Kebab
La nuit semble propice
À concocter un poème relevé
De sauce samouraï...

In the shadow of your shadow
Over the ruins of cities
I dance girded with wounds
With your evanescent corpse ever from
My mouth dripping blood
My severed tongue attempts
The unsayable while the sirens
Wail as one the emergency
In the zone with this air of ghetto
I sink into the fog
Dampened by the halos of neon lights
Under the Kebab sign
This night seems propitious
For dreaming up a poem
With notes of Samurai Sauce

Glossary

(In order of appearance)

Encre levée is a pun, because "ancre" (anchor) is a homophone of "ink."

Abu Sofiane (also Abu Sufyan) was the leader of the Quraysh, a powerful tribe in Mecca and (pre-Islamic) Arabia.

Kaaba (also Kaâba) is the Black Stone, in Mecca.

kiswa is the cloth at the Kaaba's base.

fitna (also fitnah) is Arabic for "trial" or "sedition," but often means strife.

Uthman, also Othman and Osman, was son-in-law and companion to Mohamed and a principal editor of the Koran.

Al Kufa, also Masjid al-Kufa, is in Kufa, Iraq.

Ctesiphon is a city on the Tigris, south of Baghdad (known for several battles and later destruction).

Muawiya was the founder and first Caliph of the Ommayad Caliphate, known for finesse as an administrator. He was tolerant, allowing solicitors much leeway, "like a hair," as he said, "stretching but not breaking."

Damas: Damascus.

Ghouta refers to parks and green space in Damascus.

A **fatwa** is an edict or pronouncement from an Islamic spiritual authority.

Quarmates, also Karmates, were a sect within Ismaelian Shiite Islam, c. 1000.

Alep: Aleppo.

Al-Hasa, also Al-Ahsa, is a giant oasis, also sometimes the name of the city Hofuf within it.

Bilal, known as the first muezzin, was a companion of Mohamed, and is thought to be the first to "call to prayer."

Zanj: The Zanj Rebellion (c. 880 CE) was against the Abbasid Caliphate.

Omeyyade, also Umayyad and Omayyad, the second caliphate formed after the death of Mohamed.

Ali, Hasan, and **Hussein** were grandsons of the Prophet.

Hachichines, also referred to as the cult of The Assassins, was an Islamic sect starting at the time of Hassan-i Sabbah (c.1050).

The **Mahdi** is a future redeemer, the ultimate leader of Islam.

Ibn Taymiyyah, also Taqi al-Din Ahmad ibn Taymiyyah, was a medieval (Sunni) Muslim theologian.

Sykes-Picot, also The Asia Minor Agreement (1916), was to settle spheres of influence (mainly British and French) after the fall of the Ottoman Empire, WWI.

Born in 1968 in El Maâzize, in the region of Khémisset, Mohamed Hmoudane is a poet, novelist and translator.
He has lived in France since 1989. His writing, tinged with rebelliousness and dark humor, is widely respected both in France and in the Arab world.
Among his other works: *Plus loin que toujours; Parole prise, parole donnée; Blanche mécanique; Incandescence; French Dream* and *Le Ciel, Hassan II et Maman France.*

Bouchaïb Maoual was born in 1959 in Ben Slimane and is a French-Moroccan sculpteur, painter and engraver.
He holds a national degree in the plastic arts from the Ecole Supérieure des Beaux-Arts de Marseille. He has made that city his place of work.
Maoual has been featured in many international biennial exhibitions of graphic arts. Working the space between painting and engraving, he has revolutionized the techniques and goals of those arts.
Maoual is one of the most prominent engravers in Morocco.

Also by Mohamed Hmoudane

Plus loin que toujours, Al Manar, 2015

Le Ciel, Hassan Il et Maman France, La Différence, 2010
  —Le Fennec, 2014

Parole prise, parole donnée, La Différence, 2007

French Dream, La Différence, 2005
  —Tarik Editions, 2010

Blanche Mécanique, La Différence, 2005

Incandescence, Al Manar, 2004

Attentat, La Différence, 2003

Poème d 'au-delà de la saison du silence, L'Harmattan, 1994

Ascension d 'un fragment nu en chute—Morsure des mots,
  L'Harmattan, 1992

DIÁLOGOS
dialogosbooks.com

Made in the USA
Monee, IL
13 May 2020